THE
NAME AND NATURE OF POETRY

THE
NAME AND NATURE
OF POETRY

BY

A. E. HOUSMAN

Kennedy Professor of Latin in the
University of Cambridge

THE LESLIE STEPHEN LECTURE
DELIVERED AT CAMBRIDGE
9 MAY 1933

NEW YORK: THE MACMILLAN COMPANY

CAMBRIDGE, ENGLAND: AT THE UNIVERSITY PRESS

1933

14230

The question should be fairly stated, how far a man can be an adequate, or even a good (so far as he goes) though inadequate critic of poetry, who is not a poet, at least *in posse*. Can he be an adequate, can he be a good critic, though not commensurate? But there is yet another distinction. Supposing he is not only not a poet, but is a bad poet! What then?

COLERIDGE, *Anima Poetae,* pp. 127f.

THE NAME AND NATURE
OF POETRY

It is my first duty to acknowledge the honour done me by those who have in their hands the appointment of the Leslie Stephen Lecturer, and to thank them for this token of their good will. My second duty is to say that I condemn their judgment and deplore their choice. It is twenty-two years to-day since I last, and first, spoke in this Senate-House; and in delivering my inaugural lecture, and telling this University what it was *not* to expect from me, I used these words.

Whether the faculty of literary criticism is the best gift that Heaven has in its treasuries I cannot say; but Heaven seems to think so, for assuredly it is the gift most charily bestowed. Orators and poets, sages and saints and heroes, if rare in comparison with blackberries, are commoner than returns of Halley's comet: literary critics are less common. And when, once in a century, or once in two centuries, the literary critic does appear—will some one in this home of mathematics tell me what are the chances that his appearance will be made among that small number of people who are called classical scholars? If this purely accidental conjunction occurred so lately as the eighteenth century in the person of Lessing, it ought to be a long while before it occurs again; and if so early a century as the twentieth is to witness it in another person, all I know is that I am not he.

In these twenty-two years I have improved in some respects and deteriorated in others; but I have not so much improved as to become a literary critic, nor so much deteriorated as to fancy that I have become one. Therefore you are not about to be addressed in that tone of authority which is appropriate to those who are, and is assumed by some of those who conceive themselves to be, literary critics. In order to hear Jehovah thundering out of Zion, or Little Bethel, you must go elsewhere.

But all my life long the best literature of

several languages has been my favourite rec-
reation; and good literature continually
read for pleasure must, let us hope, do some
good to the reader: must quicken his perception though dull, and sharpen his dis-
crimination though blunt, and mellow the
rawness of his personal opinions. But personal opinions they remain, not truths to
be imparted as such with the sureness of
superior insight and knowledge. I hope
however that for brevity's sake, and your
own, you will accept the disclaimer once
for all, and that when hereafter I may say
that things are thus or thus, you will not
insist on my saying instead that I humbly
venture to conceive them so or that I diffi-
dently offer the suggestion to your better
judgment.

There is indeed one literary subject on
which I think I could discourse with profit,
because it is also scientific, so that a man of
science can handle it without presumption,
and indeed is fitter for the task than most
men of letters. The Artifice of Versification, which I first thought of taking for my

[3]

theme to-day, has underlying it a set of facts which are unknown to most of those who practise it; and their success, when they succeed, is owing to instinctive tact and a natural goodness of ear. This latent base, comprising natural laws by which all versification is conditioned, and the secret springs of the pleasure which good versification can give, is little explored by critics: a few pages of Coventry Patmore and a few of Frederic Myers contain all, so far as I know, or all of value, which has been written on such matters; [1] and to these

[1] I mean such matters as these: the existence in some metres, not in others, of an inherent alternation of stresses, stronger and weaker; the presence in verse of silent and invisible feet, like rests in music; the reason why some lines of different length will combine harmoniously while others can only be so combined by great skill or good luck; why, while blank verse can be written in lines of ten or six syllables, a series of octosyllables ceases to be verse if they are not rhymed; how Coleridge, in applying the new principle which he announced in the preface to Christabel, has fallen between two stools; the necessary limit to inversion of stress, which Milton understood and Bridges overstepped; why, of two pairs of rhymes, equally correct and both consisting of the same vowels and consonants, one is richer to the mental ear and the other poorer; the office of alliteration in verse, and how its definition must be narrowed if it is to be something which can perform that office and not fail of its effect or actually defeat its purpose.

pages I could add a few more. But they would not make a good lecture: first, because of their fewness; secondly, because of their dryness; and thirdly, because they might not be easy for listeners to follow, and what I had to say would be more clearly communicated by writing than by speech. For these reasons I renounced my first intention, and chose instead a subject much less precise, and therefore less suitable to my capacity, but yet one which may be treated, as I hope to treat it, with some degree of precision.

When one begins to discuss the nature of poetry, the first impediment in the way is the inherent vagueness of the name, and the number of its legitimate senses. It is not bad English to speak of 'prose and poetry' in the sense of 'prose and verse.' But it is wasteful; it squanders a valuable word by stretching it to fit a meaning which is accurately expressed by a wider term. Verse may be, like the Tale of Sir Thopas in the judgment of Our Host of the Tabard, 'rym dogerel'; and the name of poetry is gener-

ally restricted to verse which can at least
be called literature, though it may differ
from prose only in its metrical form, and
be superior to prose only in the superior
comeliness of that form itself, and the superior terseness which usually goes along
with it. Then further there is verse which
gives a positive and lively pleasure arising
from the talent and accomplishment of its
author.

> Now Gilpin had a pleasant wit
>   And loved a timely joke,
> And thus unto the Callender
>   In merry guise he spoke:
>
> I came because your horse would come;
>   And, if I well forbode,
> My hat and wig will soon be here:
>   They are upon the road.

Capital: but no one, if asked for a typical
example of poetry, would recite those verses
in reply. A typical example need not be any
less plain and simple and straightforward,
but it would be a little raised.

> Come, worthy Greek, Ulysses, come,
>   Possess these shores with me:

The winds and seas are troublesome,
   And here we may be free.
Here may we sit and view their toil
   That travail in the deep,
And joy the day in mirth the while,
   And spend the night in sleep.

There we are ceasing to gallop with the Callender's horse and beginning to fly with Pegasus. Indeed a promising young poetaster could not do better than lay up that stanza in his memory, not necessarily as a pattern to set before him, but as a touchstone to keep at his side. Diction and movement alike, it is perfect. It is made out of the most ordinary words, yet it is pure from the least alloy of prose; and however much nearer heaven the art of poetry may have mounted, it has never flown on a surer or a lighter wing.

It is perfect, I say; and nothing more than perfection can be demanded of anything: yet poetry is capable of more than this, and more therefore is expected from it. There is a conception of poetry which is not fulfilled by pure language and liquid versification, with the simple and so to speak colourless pleasure which they afford, but involves the presence in them of something which moves and touches in a special and recognisable way. Set beside that stanza of Daniel's these lines from Bruce's or Logan's Cuckoo:

> Sweet bird, thy bower is ever green,
>   Thy sky is ever clear;
> Thou hast no sorrow in thy song,
>   No winter in thy year.

There a new element has stolen in, a tinge of emotion. And I think that to transfuse emotion—not to transmit thought but to set up in the reader's sense a vibration corresponding to what was felt by the writer—is the peculiar function of poetry. Even where the verse is not thus beautiful and engaging in its external form, as in Johnson's lines,

> His virtues walked their narrow round,
>   Nor made a pause, nor left a void;
> And sure the Eternal Master found
>   The single talent well employed,

it may yet possess the same virtue and elicit a like response.

Further than this I will not now ascend the stair of poetry. I have chosen these two examples because they may almost be called humble, and contain hardly more than the promise of what poetry attains to be. Here it is not lofty or magnificent or intense; it does not transport with rapture nor over-whelm with awe; it does not stab the heart nor shake the soul nor take the breath away. But it is poetry, though not in the highest, yet in the highest definable sense.

> Duncan is in his grave;
> After life's fitful fever he sleeps well.

Even for that poetry there is no other name.

I said that the legitimate meanings of the word poetry were themselves so many as to embarrass the discussion of its nature. All the more reason why we should not con-found confusion worse by wresting the term to licentious use and affixing it either to dissimilar things already provided with names of their own, or to new things for which new names should be invented.

There was a whole age of English in which the place of poetry was usurped by something very different which possessed the proper and specific name of wit: wit not in its modern sense, but as defined by Johnson, 'a combination of dissimilar images, or discovery of occult resemblances in things apparently unlike.' Such discoveries are no more poetical than anagrams; such pleasure as they give is purely intellectual and is intellectually frivolous; but this was the pleasure principally sought and found in poems by the intelligentsia of fifty years and more of the seventeenth century. Some of the writers who purveyed it to their contemporaries were, by accident, considerable poets; and though their verse was generally inharmonious, and apparently cut into lengths and tied into faggots by deaf mathematicians, some little of their poetry was beautiful and even superb. But it was not by this that they captivated and sought to captivate. Simile and meta-

phor, things inessential to poetry, were
their great engrossing pre-occupation, and
were prized the more in proportion as they
were further fetched. They did not mean
these accessories to be helpful, to make
their sense clearer or their conceptions
more vivid; they hardly even meant them
for ornament, or cared whether an image
had any independent power to please: their
object was to startle by novelty and amuse
by ingenuity a public whose one wish was
to be so startled and amused. The pleasure,
however luxurious, of hearing St Mary
Magdalene's eyes described as

Two walking baths, two weeping motions,
Portable and compendious oceans,

was not a poetic pleasure; and poetry, as a
label for this particular commodity, is not
appropriate.

Appropriateness is even more carefully
to be considered when the thing which we
so much admire that we wish to give it the
noblest name we can lay our tongue to is a
new thing. We should beware of treating

the word poetry as chemists have treated the word salt. Salt is a crystalline substance recognised by its taste; its name is as old as the English language and is the possession of the English people, who know what it means: it is not the private property of a science less than three hundred years old, which, being in want of a term to embody a new conception, 'an acid having the whole or part of its hydrogen replaced by a metal,' has lazily helped itself to the old and unsuitable word salt, instead of excogitating a new and therefore to that extent an apt one. The right model for imitation is that chemist who, when he encountered, or thought he had encountered, a hitherto nameless form of matter, did not purloin for it the name of something else, but invented out of his own head a name which should be proper to it, and enriched the vocabulary of modern man with the useful word *gas*. If we apply 'the word poetry to an object which does not resemble, either in form or content, anything which has heretofore been so called, not only are we maltreating and corrupting language, but we may be guilty of disrespect and blasphemy. Poetry may be too mean a name for the object in question: the object, being certainly something different, may possibly be something superior. When the Lord rained bread from heaven so that man did eat angels' food, and the children of Israel saw upon the face of the wilderness a small round thing, as small as the hoar frost on the ground, they did not call it quails: they rose to the occasion and said to one another 'it is manna.'

There is also such a thing as sham poetry, a counterfeit deliberately manufactured and offered as a substitute. In English the great historical example is certain verse produced abundantly and applauded by high and low in what for literary purposes is loosely called the eighteenth century: not a hundred years accidentally begun and ended by chronology, but a longer period which is a unity and a reality; the period lying between Samson Agonistes in 1671 and the Lyrical Ballads in 1798, and including as an integral part and indeed as its most potent influence the mature work of Dryden.

Matthew Arnold more than fifty years ago, in speaking of Wordsworth's and Coleridge's low estimate of the poetry of the eighteenth century, issued the warning 'there are many signs to show that the eighteenth century and its judgments are coming into favour again.' I remember thinking to myself that surely this could never be; but there you see what it is to be a literary critic. There has now for a good many years been a strong disposition to revise the verdict pronounced by the nineteenth century on the poetry of the eighteenth and to represent that its disparaging judgment was no more than an expression of distaste for a sort of poetry unlike its own. That is a misconception. It set a low value on the poetry of the eighteenth century, not because it differed in kind from its own, but because, even at its best, it differed in quality, as its own best poetry did not differ, from the poetry of all those ages,

[14]

whether modern or ancient, English or foreign, which are acknowledged as the great ages of poetry. Tried by that standard the poetry of the eighteenth century, even when not vicious, even when sound and good, fell short.

The literature of the eighteenth century in England is an admirable and most enjoyable thing. It has a greater solidity of excellence than any before or after; and although the special task and characteristic achievement of the age was the invention and establishment of a healthy, workmanlike, athletic prose, to supersede the cumbrous and decorated and self-admiring prose of a Milton or a Jeremy Taylor, and to become a trustworthy implement for accurate thinking and the serious pursuit of truth, yet in verse also it created masterpieces, and perhaps no English poem of greater than lyric length, not even the Nonne's Priest's Tale or the Ancient Mariner, is quite so perfect as the Rape of the Lock. But the human faculty which dominated the eighteenth century and informed

[15]

its literature was the intelligence, and that involved, as Arnold says, 'some repressing and silencing of poetry,' 'some touch of frost to the imaginative life of the soul.' Man had ceased to live from the depths of his nature; he occupied himself for choice with thoughts which do not range beyond the sphere of the understanding; he lighted the candles and drew down the blind to shut out that patroness of poets, the moon. The writing of poetry proceeded, and much of the poetry written was excellent literature; but excellent literature which is also poetry is not therefore excellent poetry, and the poetry of the eighteenth century was most satisfactory when it did not try to be poetical. Eighteenth-century poetry is in fact a name for two different things, which ought to be kept distinct. There was a good sound workaday article, efficiently discharging a worthy and honourable though not an exalted duty. Satire, controversy, and burlesque, to which the eighteenth century was drawn by the character of its genius, and in which its achievement was unrivalled, are forms of art in which high poetry is not at home, and to which, unless introduced with great parsimony and tact, it would be actually injurious and disfiguring. The conclusion of the Dunciad may fairly be called sublime; but such a tone was wisely reserved for the conclusion. The modicum of the poetical element which satire can easily accommodate is rather what we find in lines like these:

Riches, like insects, when conceal'd they lie,
Wait but for wings, and in their season fly.
Who sees pale Mammon pine amidst his store
Sees but a backward steward for the poor:
This year a reservoir, to keep and spare;
The next, a fountain, spouting through his
        heir,
In lavish streams to quench a country's thirst,
And men and dogs shall drink him till they
        burst.

And what sterling stuff they are! But such writing, which was their true glory and should have been their proper pride, did not content its writers. They felt that this, after all, did not rank as equal with the po-

[17]

etry of other ages, nor fulfil the conception of poetry which was obscurely present in their minds; and they aspired to something which should be less pedestrian. It was as though the ostrich should attempt to fly. The ostrich on her own element is the swiftest of created things; she scorneth the horse and his rider; and although we are also told that God hath deprived her of wisdom, neither hath he imparted to her understanding, he has at any rate given her sense enough to know that she is not a lark or an eagle. To poets of the eighteenth century high and impassioned poetry did not come spontaneously, because the feelings which foster its birth were not then abundant and urgent in the inner man; but they girt up their loins and essayed a lofty strain at the bidding of ambition. The way to write real poetry, they thought, must be to write something as little like prose as possible; they devised for the purpose what was called a 'correct and splendid diction,' which consisted in always using the wrong word instead of the right, and plastered it as ornament, with no thought of propriety, on whatever they desired to dignify. It commanded notice and was not easy to mistake; so the public mind soon connected it with the notion of poetry and came in course of time to regard it as alone poetical.[1]

It was in truth at once pompous and poverty-stricken. It had a very limited, be-

---

[1] It is now customary to say that the nineteenth century had a similar lingo of its own. A lingo it had, or came to have, and in the seventies and eighties the minor poets and poetasters were all using the same supposedly poetic diction. It was imitative and sapless, but not preposterous: its leading characteristic was a stale and faded prettiness.

> As one that for a weary space has lain
>   Lull'd by the song of Circe and her wine
>   In gardens near the pale of Proserpine,
> Where that Æean isle forgets the main,
> And only the low lutes of love complain,
>   And only shadows of wan lovers pine—
>   As such an one were glad to know the brine
> Salt on his lips, and the large air again. . . .

The atmosphere of the eighteenth century made much better poets write much worse.

> Lo! where the rosy-bosom'd Hours,
>   Fair Venus' train, appear,
> Disclose the long-expecting flowers
>   And wake the purple year!
> The Attic warbler pours her throat

and so forth.

[19]

cause supposedly choice, vocabulary, and was consequently unequal to the multitude and refinement of its duties. It could not describe natural objects with sensitive fidelity to nature; it could not express human feelings with a variety and delicacy answering to their own. A thick, stiff, unaccommodating medium was interposed between the writer and his work. And this deadening of language had a consequence beyond its own sphere: its effect worked inward, and deadened perception. That which could no longer be described was no longer noticed.

The features and formation of the style can be studied under a cruel light in Dryden's translations from Chaucer. The Knight's Tale of Palamon and Arcite is not one of Chaucer's most characteristic and successful poems: he is not perfectly at home, as in the Prologue and the tale of Chauntecleer and Pertelote, and his movement is a trifle languid. Dryden's translation shows Dryden in the maturity of his power and accomplishment, and much of it can be honestly and soberly admired. Nor was he insensible to all the peculiar excellence of Chaucer: he had the wit to keep unchanged such lines as 'Up rose the sun and up rose Emily' or 'The slayer of himself yet saw I there'; he understood that neither he nor anyone else could better them. But much too often in a like case he would try to improve, because he thought that he could. He believed, as he says himself, that he was 'turning some of the Canterbury Tales into our language, as it is now refined'; 'the words' he says again 'are given up as a post not to be defended in our poet, because he wanted the modern art of fortifying'; 'in some places' he tells us 'I have added somewhat of my own where I thought my author was deficient, and had not given his thoughts their true lustre, for want of words in the beginning of our language.'

Let us look at the consequences. Chaucer's vivid and memorable line

The smiler with the knife under the cloke

becomes these three:

> Next stood Hypocrisy, with holy leer,
> Soft smiling and demurely looking down,
> But hid the dagger underneath the gown.

Again:

> Alas, quod he, that day that I was bore.

So Chaucer, for want of words in the beginning of our language. Dryden comes to his assistance and gives his thoughts their true lustre thus:

Cursed be the day when first I did appear;
Let it be blotted from the calendar,
Lest it pollute the month and poison all the
year.

Or yet again:

> The queen anon for very womanhead
> Gan for to weep, and so did Emily
> And all the ladies in the company.

If Homer or Dante had the same thing to say, would he wish to say it otherwise? But to Dryden Chaucer wanted the modern art of fortifying, which he thus applies:

[22]

He said; dumb sorrow seized the standers-by.
The queen, above the rest, by nature good
(The pattern formed of perfect womanhood)
For tender pity wept: when she began
Through the bright quire the infectious vir-
    tue ran.
All dropped their tears, even the contended
    maid.

Had there not fallen upon England the curse out of Isaiah, 'make the heart of this people fat, and make their ears heavy, and shut their eyes'? That there should ever have existed an obtuseness which could mistake this impure verbiage for a correct and splendid diction is a dreadful thought. More dreadful is the experience of seeing it poured profusely, continually, and with evident exultation, from the pen of a great and deservedly illustrious author. But most dreadful of all is the reflexion that he was himself its principal origin. The correctness of calling Emily 'the contended maid' is his correctness, and the splendour of 'through the bright quire the infectious virtue ran' is his own infectious vice. His

disciple Pope admired this line so much
that he put it twice into his Iliad.

Through all her train the soft infection ran.

The infectious softness through the heroes
ran.

This same Dryden, when his self-cor-
rupted taste and the false guidance of ambition would let him, could write in verse
even better than he wrote in prose, dipping
his bucket in the same well of pure, whole-
some, racy English. What a joy it is to whis-
tle correctness and splendour down the
wind, and hear him speak out straight in
the vernacular.

Till frowning skies began to change their
    cheer,
And time turned up the wrong side of the
    year.

Bare benting times and moulting months may
    come,
When lagging late they cannot reach their
    home.

Your benefices twinkled from afar;
They found the new Messiah by the star.

And not only in his domestic sphere of satire and controversy but in this very book of Fables, where he is venturing abroad. To his translation of the Flower and the Leaf he prefixed these nineteen lines of his own.

Now, turning from the wintry signs, the Sun
His course exalted through the Ram had run,
And whirling up the skies his chariot drove
Through Taurus and the lightsome realms of
     Love,
Where Venus from her orb descends in
     showers
To glad the ground and paint the fields
     with flowers:
When first the tender blades of grass appear
And buds that yet the blast of Eurus fear
Stand at the door of life and doubt to clothe
     the year,
Till gentle heat and soft repeated rains
Make the green blood to dance within their
     veins.
Then at their call emboldened out they come
And swell the gems and burst the narrow
     room,
Broader and broader yet their blooms display,
Salute the welcome sun and entertain the day.

Then from their breathing souls the sweets
    repair
To scent the skies and purge the unwhole-
    some air:
Joy spreads the heart, and with a general song
Spring issues out and leads the jolly months
    along.

What exuberant beauty and vigour! and what nature! I believe that I admire that passage more heartily and relish it more keenly than Pope or Johnson or Dryden's own contemporaries could, because I live outside their dungeon, the dungeon in which Dryden himself had shut them up; because my ears are not contentedly attuned to the choir of captives singing hymns in the prison chapel, but can listen to the wild music that burdens every bough in the free world outside the wall.

Not that even this passage will quite sustain that comparison. When I am drinking Barolo stravecchio in Turin, I am not disturbed, nor even visited, by the reflexion that there is better wine in Dijon. But yet there is; and there was better poetry, not reckoning Milton's, even in the perverse and crooked generation preceding Dryden. Thinly scattered on that huge dross-heap, the Caroline Parnassus, there were tiny gems of purer ray; and the most genuine of Dryden's own poetry is to be found, never more than four lines at once, seldom more than two, in his early, unshapely, and wearisome poem the Annus Mirabilis.

His great successor, whose Iliad was a more dazzling and seductive example of the false manner than any work of Dryden's own, and became, as Coleridge said, 'the main source of our pseudo-poetic diction' —Pope, though he threw open to others the wide gate, did not long keep them company on the broad way, which led them to destruction. He came to recognise, and for the last twenty years of his life he steadily followed, the true bent of his genius, in satire or disputation: into these he put no larger quantity and no rarer quality of poetry than they would assimilate, and he made no more ascents in the balloon. Pope had less of the poetic gift than Dryden; in common with his contemporaries he drew from a poorer vocabulary; and his versification, though more evenly good, did not reach the buoyant excellence of Dryden's at its best. What lifts him nearest to true poetry is sincere inward ardour. Pope had a soul in his body, an aery and fiery particle, where Dryden had nothing but a lump of clay, and he can be nobler than Dryden can. But not even in the Elegy to the memory of an unfortunate lady does the fire burn clear of smoke, and truth of emotion do itself full justice in naturalness and purity of diction.

Nuns fret not at their convent's narrow room, and the eighteenth century, except for a few malcontents, was satisfied with what its leading poets provided. 'It is surely superfluous' says Johnson 'to answer the question that has once been asked, whether Pope was a poet, otherwise than by asking in return, if Pope be not a poet, where is poetry to be found?' It is to be found, Dr Johnson, in Dr Watts.

> Soft and easy is thy cradle;
>> Coarse and hard thy Saviour lay,
> When his birthplace was a stable
> And his softest bed was hay.

That simple verse, bad rhyme and all, is poetry beyond Pope. It is to be found again, Samuel, in your namesake Benjamin, as tough a piece of timber as yourself.

> What gentle ghost, besprent with April dew,
> Hails me so solemnly to yonder yew,
> And beckoning woos me, from the fatal tree,
> To pluck a garland for herself or me?

When Pope imitated that, he got no nearer than this:

> What beck'ning ghost along the moon-light
>> shade
> Invites my steps and points to yonder glade?
> 'Tis she!—but why that bleeding bosom gor'd,
>> etc.

When I hear anyone say, with defiant emphasis, that Pope was a poet, I suspect him of calling in ambiguity of language to promote confusion of thought. That Pope was a poet is true; but it is one of those truths which are beloved of liars, because they serve so well the cause of falsehood. That Pope was not a poet is false; but a righteous man, standing in awe of the last judgment and the lake which burneth with fire and brimstone, might well prefer to say it.

It is impossible to admire such poetry as Pope's so whole-heartedly as Johnson did, and to rest in it with such perfect contentment, without losing the power to appreciate finer poetry or even to recognise it when met. Johnson's unlucky frankness in letting the world know how he was affected by Lycidas has earned his critical judgment discredit enough; but consider also his response to poetry which, though somehow written in the eighteenth century, is of an alien strain and worthy of other ages; consider his attitude to Collins. For Collins himself he felt esteem and liking, and his kind heart must have made him wish to speak well of his friend's poetry; but he was an honest man, and could not.

The first impediment, I said, to dealing with the subject of poetry is the native ambiguity of the term. But the course of these remarks has now brought us to a point where another and perhaps greater difficulty awaits us in determining the competence or incompetence of the judge, that is the sensibility or insensibility of the percipient. Am I capable of recognising poetry if I come across it? Do I possess the organ by which poetry is perceived? The majority of civilised mankind notoriously and indisputably do not; who has certified me that I am one of the minority who do? I may know what I like and admire, I may like and admire it intensely; but what makes me think that it is poetry? Is my reason for thinking so anything more than this: that poetry is generally esteemed the highest form of literature, and that my opinion of myself forbids me to believe that what I most like and admire is anything short of the highest? Yet why be unwilling to admit that perhaps you cannot perceive poetry? Why think it necessary to your self-respect that you should? How many of the good and great, how many saints and heroes have possessed this faculty? Can you hear the shriek of the bat? Probably not; but do you think the less of yourself on that account? do you pretend to others, or even try to persuade yourself, that you can? Is it an unbearable thing, and crushing to self-conceit, to be in the majority?

If a man is insensible to poetry, it does not follow that he gets no pleasure from poems. Poems very seldom consist of poetry and nothing else; and pleasure can be derived also from their other ingredients. I am convinced that most readers, when they think that they are admiring poetry, are deceived by inability to analyse their sensations, and that they are really admiring, not the poetry of the passage before them, but something else in it, which they like better than poetry.

To begin with a very obvious instance. I have been told by devout women that to them the most beautiful poetry is Keble's. Keble is a poet; there are things in the Christian Year which can be admired by atheists; but what devout women most prize in it, as Keble himself would have wished, is not its poetry; and I much doubt whether any of them, if asked to pick out the best poem in the book, would turn at once to the Second Sunday after Easter. Good religious poetry, whether in Keble or Dante or Job, is likely to be most justly appreciated and most discriminatingly relished by the undevout.

Again, there existed in the last century a great body of Wordsworthians, as they were called. It is now much smaller; but true appreciation of Wordsworth's poetry has not diminished in proportion: I suspect that it has much increased. The Wordsworthians, as Matthew Arnold told them, were apt to praise their poet for the wrong things. They were most attracted by what may be called his philosophy; they accepted his belief in the morality of the universe and the tendency of events to good; they were even willing to entertain his conception of nature as a living and sentient and benignant being, a conception as purely mythological as the Dryads and the Naiads.

[33] \4230

To that thrilling utterance which pierces the heart and brings tears to the eyes of thousands who care nothing for his opinions and beliefs they were not noticeably sensitive; and however justly they admired the depth of his insight into human nature and the nobility of his moral ideas, these things, with which his poetry was in close and harmonious alliance, are distinct from poetry itself.

When I examine my mind and try to discern clearly in the matter, I cannot satisfy myself that there are any such things as poetical ideas. No truth, it seems to me, is too precious, no observation too profound, and no sentiment too exalted to be expressed in prose. The utmost that I could admit is that some ideas do, while others do not, lend themselves kindly to poetical expression; and that these receive from poetry an enhancement which glorifies and almost transfigures them, and which is not perceived to be a separate thing except by analysis.

'Whosoever will save his life shall lose it,

and whosoever will lose his life shall find it.' That is the most important truth which has ever been uttered, and the greatest discovery ever made in the moral world; but I do not find in it anything which I should call poetical. On the other hand, when Wisdom says in the Proverbs 'He that sinneth against me wrongeth his own soul; all they that hate me, love death,' that is to me poetry, because of the words in which the idea is clothed; and as for the seventh verse of the forty-ninth Psalm in the Book of Common Prayer, 'But no man may deliver his brother, nor make agreement unto God for him,' that is to me poetry so moving that I can hardly keep my voice steady in reading it. And that this is the effect of language I can ascertain by experiment: the same thought in the bible version, 'None of them can by any means redeem his brother, nor give to God a ransom for him,' I can read without emotion.

Poetry is not the thing said but a way of saying it. Can it then be isolated and studied by itself? for the combination of language with its intellectual content, its meaning, is as close a union as can well be imagined. Is there such a thing as pure unmingled poetry, poetry independent of meaning?

Even when poetry has a meaning, as it usually has, it may be inadvisable to draw it out. 'Poetry gives most pleasure' said Coleridge 'when only generally and not perfectly understood'; and perfect understanding will sometimes almost extinguish pleasure. The Haunted Palace is one of Poe's best poems so long as we are content to swim in the sensations it evokes and only vaguely to apprehend the allegory. We are roused to discomfort, at least I am, when we begin to perceive how exact in detail the allegory is; when it dawns upon us that the fair palace door is Roderick Usher's mouth, the pearl and ruby his teeth and lips, the yellow banners his hair, the ramparts plumed and pallid his forehead, and when we are reduced to hoping, for it is no more than a hope, that the wingèd odours have no connexion with hair-oil.

Meaning is of the intellect, poetry is not.
If it were, the eighteenth century would
have been able to write it better. As matters actually stand, who are the English
poets of that age in whom pre-eminently
one can hear and recognise the true poetic
accent emerging clearly from the contem-
porary dialect? These four: Collins, Chris-
topher Smart, Cowper, and Blake. And
what other characteristic had these four in
common? They were mad. Remember
Plato: 'He who without the Muses' mad-
ness in his soul comes knocking at the door
of poesy and thinks that art will make him
anything fit to be called a poet, finds that
the poetry which he indites in his sober
senses is beaten hollow by the poetry of
madmen.'

That the intellect is not the fount of
poetry, that it may actually hinder its production, and that it cannot even be trusted
to recognise poetry when produced, is best
seen in the case of Smart. Neither the prize
founded in this University by the Rev.
Thomas Seaton nor the successive contem-

plation of five several attributes of the Su-
preme Being could incite him to good
poetry while he was sane. The only poem
by which he is remembered, a poem which
came to its own in the kinder climate of the
nineteenth century and has inspired one
of the best poems of the twentieth, was
written, if not, as tradition says, in actual
confinement, at any rate very soon after re-
lease; and when the eighteenth century,
the age of sanity and intelligence, collected
his poetical works, it excluded this piece as
'bearing melancholy proofs of the recent
estrangement of his mind.'

Collins and Cowper, though they saw the
inside of madhouses, are not supposed to
have written any of their poetry there; and
Blake was never mad enough to be locked
up. But elements of their nature were
more or less insurgent against the central-
ised tyranny of the intellect, and their
brains were not thrones on which the great
usurper could sit secure. And so it strangely
came to pass that in the eighteenth century, the age of prose and of unsound or

[38]

unsatisfying poetry, there sprang up one well of the purest inspiration. For me the most poetical of all poets is Blake. I find his lyrical note as beautiful as Shakespeare's and more beautiful than anyone else's; and I call him more poetical than Shakespeare, even though Shakespeare has so much more poetry, because poetry in him preponderates more than in Shakespeare over everything else, and instead of being confounded in a great river can be drunk pure from a slender channel of its own. Shakespeare is rich in thought, and his meaning has power of itself to move us, even if the poetry were not there: Blake's meaning is often unimportant or virtually non-existent, so that we can listen with all our hearing to his celestial tune.

Even Shakespeare, who had so much to say, would sometimes pour out his loveliest poetry in saying nothing.

Take O take those lips away
That so sweetly were forsworn,
And those eyes, the break of day,
Lights that do mislead the morn;

But my kisses bring again,
              bring again,
Seals of love, but seal'd in vain,
              seal'd in vain.

That is nonsense; but it is ravishing poetry. When Shakespeare fills such poetry with thought, and thought which is worthy of it, as in *Fear no more the heat o' the sun* or *O mistress mine, where art thou roaming?* those songs, the very summits of lyrical achievement, are indeed greater and more moving poems, but I hardly know how to call them more poetical.

Now Blake again and again, as Shakespeare now and then, gives us poetry neat, or adulterated with so little meaning that nothing except poetic emotion is perceived and matters.

Hear the voice of the Bard,
   Who present, past, and future sees;
Whose ears have heard
The Holy Word
   That walk'd among the ancient trees,

Calling the lapsèd soul
   And weeping in the evening dew;

[40]

That might control
The starry pole,
  And fallen, fallen light renew.

'O Earth, O Earth, return!
  Arise from out the dewy grass;
Night is worn,
And the morn
  Rises from the slumberous mass.

'Turn away no more;
  Why wilt thou turn away?
The starry floor,
The watery shore
  Is giv'n thee till the break of day.'

That mysterious grandeur would be less grand if it were less mysterious; if the embryo ideas which are all that it contains should endue form and outline, and suggestion condense itself into thought.

Memory, hither come
  And tune your merry notes;
And while upon the wind
  Your music floats

I'll pore upon the stream
Where sighing lovers dream,
And fish for fancies as they pass
Within the watery glass.

[41]

That answers to nothing real; memory's
merry notes and the rest are empty phrases,
not things to be imagined; the stanza does
but entangle the reader in a net of thought-
less delight. The verses which I am now
going to read probably possessed for Blake
a meaning, and his students think that they
have found it; but the meaning is a poor
foolish disappointing thing in comparison
with the verses themselves.

> My Spectre around me night and day
> Like a wild beast guards my way;
> My Emanation far within
> Weeps incessantly for my sin.
>
> A fathomless and boundless deep,
> There we wander, there we weep;
> On the hungry craving wind
> My Spectre follows thee behind.
>
> He scents thy footsteps in the snow
> Wheresoever thou dost go:
> Through the wintry hail and rain
> When wilt thou return again?
>
> Dost thou not in pride and scorn
> Fill with tempests all my morn,

And with jealousies and fears
Fill my pleasant nights with tears?

Seven of my sweet loves thy knife
Has bereavèd of their life.
Their marble tombs I built with tears
And with cold and shuddering fears.

Seven more loves weep night and day
Round the tombs where my loves lay,
And seven more loves attend each night
Around my couch with torches bright.

And seven more loves in my bed
Crown with wine my mournful head,
Pitying and forgiving all
Thy transgressions great and small.

When wilt thou return and view
My loves, and them to life renew?
When wilt thou return and live?
When wilt thou pity as I forgive?

I am not equal to framing definite ideas
which would match that magnificent versification and correspond to the strong
tremor of unreasonable excitement which
those words set up in some region deeper
than the mind. Lastly take this stanza, ad-

dressed 'to the Accuser who is the God of this World.'

Tho' thou art worship'd by the names divine
  Of Jesus and Jehovah, thou art still
The Son of Morn in weary Night's decline,
  The lost traveller's dream under the hill.

It purports to be theology: what theological sense, if any, it may have, I cannot imagine and feel no wish to learn: it is pure and self-existent poetry, which leaves no room in me for anything besides.

In most poets, as I said, poetry is less often found thus disengaged from its usual concomitants, from certain things with which it naturally unites itself and seems to blend indistinguishably. For instance:

Sorrow, that is not sorrow, but delight;
And miserable love, that is not pain
To hear of, for the glory that redounds
Therefrom to human kind, and what we are.

The feeling with which those lines are read is composite, for one constituent is supplied by the depth and penetrating truth of the thought. Again:

[44]

Though love repine and reason chafe,
    There came a voice without reply,—
' 'Tis man's perdition to be safe,
    When for the truth he ought to die.'

Much of the emotion kindled by that verse
can be referred to the nobility of the sentiment. But in these six simple words of
Milton—

Nymphs and shepherds, dance no more—

what is it that can draw tears, as I know it
can, to the eyes of more readers than one?
What in the world is there to cry about?
Why have the mere words the physical effect of pathos when the sense of the passage
is blithe and gay? I can only say, because
they are poetry, and find their way to something in man which is obscure and latent,
something older than the present organisa-
tion of his nature, like the patches of fen
which still linger here and there in the
drained lands of Cambridgeshire.

Poetry indeed seems to me more physical
than intellectual. A year or two ago, in
common with others, I received from

America a request that I would define poetry. I replied that I could no more define poetry than a terrier can define a rat, but that I thought we both recognised the object by the symptoms which it provokes in us. One of these symptoms was described in connexion with another object by Eliphaz the Temanite: 'A spirit passed before my face: the hair of my flesh stood up.' Experience has taught me, when I am shaving of a morning, to keep watch over my thoughts, because, if a line of poetry strays into my memory, my skin bristles so that the razor ceases to act. This particular symptom is accompanied by a shiver down the spine; there is another which consists in a constriction of the throat and a precipitation of water to the eyes; and there is a third which I can only describe by borrowing a phrase from one of Keats's last letters, where he says, speaking of Fanny Brawne, 'everything that reminds me of her goes through me like a spear.' The seat of this sensation is the pit of the stomach.

My opinions on poetry are necessarily

tinged, perhaps I should say tainted, by the circumstance that I have come into contact with it on two sides. We were saying a while ago that poetry is a very wide term, and inconveniently comprehensive: so comprehensive is it that it embraces two books, fortunately not large ones, of my own. I know how this stuff came into existence; and though I have no right to assume that any other poetry came into existence in the same way, yet I find reason to believe that some poetry, and quite good poetry, did. Wordsworth for instance says that poetry is the spontaneous overflow of powerful feelings, and Burns has left us this confession, 'I have two or three times in my life composed from the wish rather than the impulse, but I never succeeded to any purpose.' In short I think that the production of poetry, in its first stage, is less an active than a passive and involuntary process; and if I were obliged, not to define poetry, but to name the class of things to which it belongs, I should call it a secretion; whether a natural secretion, like turpentine in the fir, or a morbid secretion, like the pearl in the oyster. I think that my own case, though I may not deal with the material so cleverly as the oyster does, is the latter; because I have seldom written poetry unless I was rather out of health, and the experience, though pleasurable, was generally agitating and exhausting. If only that you may know what to avoid, I will give some account of the process.

Having drunk a pint of beer at luncheon —beer is a sedative to the brain, and my afternoons are the least intellectual portion of my life—I would go out for a walk of two or three hours. As I went along, thinking of nothing in particular, only looking at things around me and following the progress of the seasons, there would flow into my mind, with sudden and unaccountable emotion, sometimes a line or two of verse, sometimes a whole stanza at once, accompanied, not preceded, by a vague notion of the poem which they were destined to form part of. Then there would usually be a lull of an hour or so, then perhaps the spring would bubble up again. I say bubble up, because, so far as I could make out, the source of the suggestions thus proffered to the brain was an abyss which I have already had occasion to mention, the pit of the stomach. When I got home I wrote them down, leaving gaps, and hoping that further inspiration might be forthcoming another day. Sometimes it was, if I took my walks in a receptive and expectant frame of mind; but sometimes the poem had to be taken in hand and completed by the brain, which was apt to be a matter of trouble and anxiety, involving trial and disappoint- ment, and sometimes ending in failure. I happen to remember distinctly the genesis of the piece which stands last in my first volume. Two of the stanzas, I do not say which, came into my head, just as they are printed, while I was crossing the corner of Hampstead Heath between the Spaniard's Inn and the footpath to Temple Fortune. A third stanza came with a little coaxing after tea. One more was needed, but it did not come: I had to turn to and compose it myself, and that was a laborious business. I wrote it thirteen times, and it was more than a twelvemonth before I got it right.

By this time you must be sated with anatomy, pathology, and autobiography, and willing to let me retire from my incursion into the foreign territory of literary criticism. Farewell for ever. I will not say with Coleridge that I recentre my immortal mind in the deep sabbath of meek self-content; but I shall go back with relief and thankfulness to my proper job.